How To Make
Iced Coffee

20 Best Iced Coffee Recipes

Jeen van der Meer

How To Make Iced Coffee

© 2012 by Jeen van der Meer

Printed in the United States of America

Learn more information at: www.coffee-makers-review.com

TABLE OF CONTENTS

INTRODUCTION

Do you enjoy coffee? How do you like it? Hot? Iced?

Iced coffee has a love hate relationship with some.
Some fearless coffee drinkers only drink it hot. They feel it is a sin to drink it any other way. Then there are those that will drink it any way they can get it--even in ice cream.

Then you have those who do not care for coffee but will drink it by the gallon if it is iced.

Which one are you?

This eBook is created for whoever loves to enjoy a nice tall glass of iced coffee right from the comforts of their own home.

Do you stop at coffee houses like Starbucks on your way to work, and pay for a cup of coffee as the entire cans costs? Drinking just one cup a day like that can really cut into a budget. However, for true addicts, this is a tough habit to break.

There is no need to break the habit when you can make these delicious cups or glasses of iced coffee right from home. For the cost of a week's worth of coffee house coffees, you can buy the ingredients for enough iced coffee for about a month.

Coffee's reputation is sometimes not so good. Nevertheless, did you know that coffee has some great benefits? Drinking a cup (or glass), a day will make you healthier in the long run.

Coffee contains anti-oxidants, and this helps to boost the immune system, helps to keep you from coming down with certain illnesses. Like anything, too much coffee is a bad thing, but in moderation, it is actually beneficial for you.

Iced coffee has its roots all over the world. People in Australia, Japan, Greece, Israel, Vietnam, USA and even China enjoy this sweet cool drink.

Iced coffee is a fad, but it is here to stay? With the many different combinations and recipes, one just has to set out to try all of them and will be drinking iced coffee for over a year without repeating the flavor.

Enjoy these delicious iced coffee recipes.

HOME COLD BREWED BASIC ICED COFFEE

Learning how to create delicious iced coffee right from home is really easy. You just need to allow some good prep time in order to create a drink that rivals those found in the famous baristas.

A real iced coffee takes time, to gather the full flavor, so when you take a sip you will instantly savor it.

Many times when people try to make iced coffee from home they end up with a drink that is either too bitter or too sweet.

The key is in finding the perfect recipe, the right amount of ingredients, and just the right touch when making it.

For this recipe, the coffee needs to be cold brewed. Put away the coffee maker, you will not need it for this brew.

If you want you can put the grounds in a coffee filter, and fill the pot with cold water.

Dip the coffee filter down into the water, and leave it soaking overnight. This keeps the coffee flavor smooth and the need for extra sugar away.

Another way to make it, just add the grounds directly to the water.

Initial cold-brewed coffee:

1/4 cup of coffee grounds (do not use the fine grounds)
1 cup of cold water (filtered water is best)

Either pour the grounds into the coffee, use the filter dipped in the water, or just add them directly to the water (preferred method). Let it sit overnight.

The following morning, add 1 more cup of cold filtered water. If you have the grounds mixed in with the water, you will want to pour the coffee through a filter or strain to pull out the grounds.

Now you are ready to create with this basic mixture.

Try adding variations of these until you find a flavor you enjoy:

Sugar
Milk
Simple syrup - vanilla or chocolate (or both)

COLD BREW VANILLA ICED COFFEE

By now you may be thinking that making an iced coffee should be as quick and easy as brewing a fresh pot of "hot" coffee, then pouring it over a tall glass of ice, and voila, iced coffee. Right?

Well, you can do this, if you like weak, watered-down coffee. You are more likely to spit this out and pour down the drain than to drink it.

If you are a lover of the brewed coffee flavor, you do not have to sacrifice your flavor just because you want it iced. Cold brewing a coffee, gives you the same wonderful full flavor of hot brewing, only this works better for the iced coffee recipes.

Cold brewing takes a while; it is not a quick fix. If you want a quick recipe, then you need to look at one of our instant recipes that call for instant coffee.

This particular recipe calls for the slow cold brew coffee. Once you taste it, you will be glad you allowed the time to make it.

Cold Brew Coffee Preparation

Pour 1/4 cup of your favorite "vanilla flavored" coffee grounds into pitcher.

Pour 1 cup of filtered water over the grounds, stir and refrigerate overnight. For best results, allow to steep for at least 10 hours.

The next morning, or after the 10 hours of steeping, pour in another cup of cold water. Stir.

Pour into another pitcher, through a coffee filter, or cheesecloth to catch the coffee grounds.

Other Ingredients

> → **Half-and-half**
> → **Milk**
> → **Sugar (or sugar substitute)**
> → **Vanilla extract**

There are no measurements, because this is the part where you will flavor to your liking. Start with about 2 tablespoons of the half-and-half in the glass.

Pour in the coffee, leaving room for however much milk you care to add.

Add in a teaspoon of sugar (more or less, depending on your tastes).

Add a splashing of the vanilla extract. Stir and enjoy.

Adjust the ingredients to your own desire.

SIMPLE COLD BREW RECIPE

PERFECT FOR THE BREWED FLAVOR, BUT INSTANT AVAILABILITY.

This recipe is for a simple cold brew coffee that you can store and keep on hand. Once you make this recipe will last for several weeks in the refrigerator.

All you will need to do is flavor it. This is a good recipe for when you will want iced coffee available quickly.

It also allows you to experiment with different flavors. It is good for the need to have it quick and convenient.

The prep time is the only time you will need for creation - that is overnight.

Make sure you have a large enough container to store the coffee, about two gallons. You can store in 2 containers in the refrigerator.

Ingredients:

➜ **1 full pound of your favorite ground coffee**
➜ **8 quarts of cold water**
➜ **Your choice of flavors - suggestions: half-and-half, sweetened condensed milk (like Eagle brand), sweetened syrups like chocolate, caramel, butterscotch, and or flavored coffee creamers.**

Pour the water into a large container (which can be a large cooking pot, something with a lid to cover while it "brews") with the coffee grounds. Stir.

Allow to sit overnight. It is okay to sit out, or if there is room you can put in refrigerator, but not necessary during the "brewing" process.

The next morning, sieve the coffee by pouring through a strainer, cheesecloth or a coffee filter. You do not want coffee grounds in the brew.

Pour the mixture into a container to store in the refrigerator for a couple of weeks (three weeks maximum, after that discard unused drink).

The coffee is ready to drink now.

Pour coffee over a tall glass of ice and add the flavoring as you like, as much or little as you like. Enjoy.

CARAMEL MOCHA ICED COFFEE

This is truly a rich and satisfying iced coffee drink. If you are a chocolate and caramel lover, this one simply combines the two into a tasty drink that needs to be called a dessert instead.

Really, you will need a spoon for this, sipping is optional. You will not regret trying this recipe and it is sure to be on your favorites for iced coffee.

This iced coffee recipe can work well as a hot beverage too, by trading ice for water. However, this is first and foremost an iced coffee recipe.

Prepare to delight your taste buds.

Ingredients

→ **1/2 cup of coffee**
→ **Dozen ice cubes**
→ **1/2 cup of milk**
→ **1/2 can of sweetened condensed milk**
→ **1 tablespoon of chocolate syrup**
→ **1 tablespoon of caramel syrup**
→ **1 dollop of whipped topping**
→ **Cocoa powder (optional garnishment)**

First, make the coffee. There are several ways to make the coffee and you need to determine which way you would like the best, which one would taste best.

The first way (and best) is to hot brew the coffee, then allow to chill in the refrigerator. Alternate methods, cold brew over night, or use instant coffee to create 1/2 cup of coffee.

Chill a tall glass in the freezer while prepping the drink.

Pour the chilled coffee into a blender along with the ice cubes, sweetened condensed milk, milk, and the chocolate and caramel syrups.

Blend until well mixed.

Pour mixture into the frosty tall glass.

Top with whipped cream and garnish with either a drizzle of chocolate or caramel syrup or a dusting of cocoa powder. (If you are daring, garnish with all three.)

Then take a spoon and enjoy!

1 serving.

Variation:

Garnish with a scoop of vanilla ice cream instead of whipped topping.

FRENCH STYLE ICED COFFEE

This delicious iced coffee recipe is tailor made for those who love the heavy creamed French foods. Heaving whipping cream makes for a rich and smooth drink.

This drink is so decadent it needs to be called a dessert instead of a drink. If you want to be really French with the recipe, make a few extra dollops of whipped cream and add to the icy drink. You may want to drink, um, eat with a spoon.

There are no set rules for iced coffee recipes, other than to mix in delicious ingredients with the actual coffee.

Another variation of this recipe is to make the coffee and put in plastic mugs, and put in freezer for an hour or so. You will need a spoon for this frozen treat, or a straw.

If you love cherries, put one on top with some additional whipped topping.

Add a dab of caramel or chocolate for a nice French twist.

Ingredients:

- → **3 cups of hot coffee**
- → **1 cup heavy whipping cream**
- → **1/4 cup of powdered sugar**
- → **1 teaspoon vanilla**
- → **crushed ice**

Make the 3 cups of hot coffee. You want the coffee hot so the whipped topping will melt into it.

Either you can use an instant or a brewed coffee, either one is fine, just make sure it is hot enough, not boiling.

Add the vanilla to the coffee. In a mixing bowl, beat the heavy shipping cream until soft peaks appear.

Fold in the powdered sugar; beat again this time forming stiff peaks.

Add equal amounts of whipped cream to 4 mugs.

Pour the coffee "over" the whipped topping.

Cool the coffee mixture completely. Put some crushed ice in the bottom of 4 glasses.

Pour the coffee mixture over the crushed ice. Enjoy.

Latte Coffee Shake

Chocolate lovers look no further than this Latte Coffee shake, for a mouth full of delicious rich chocolate, and coffee.

This dessert quality iced coffee can take a nice big dollop of whipped cream on top, and even a cherry, if you dare!

The pudding is what makes this drink so rich, think, and decadent. You definitely want to keep a spoon handy; it is reminiscent of a thick milk shake.

Make it extra special, after you blend the shake and pour into a tall glass, top with whipped cream, and sprinkle a little cocoa powder over the top.

This drink is excellent for any time of day, if you like to start the day with a cup of coffee, try the frozen treat instead, especially if it is summer time.

It is so rich it can definitely be called a dessert, or a very delicious snack.

Other variations, add a bit of caramel syrup. Drizzle caramel over the whipped topping. Drizzle chocolate syrup over the whipped topping.

You can be double daring with the shake and you can drizzle both chocolate and caramel over the whipped topping.

Ingredients:

- → **1 cup strong coffee**
- → **1 cup milk**
- → **12 ice cubes**
- → **1/3 package of instant chocolate pudding**
- → **2 tablespoons of cocoa powder**
- → **Hazelnut creamer (or your favorite kind, just a splash for taste)**
- → **Sugar (to sweeten, however much you enjoy)**
- → **Whipped topping (optional)**

This Latte Coffee shake is one of the super easy recipes. Prepare coffee ahead of time. You can brew a hot cup, then chill, or use instant coffee.

On the other hand, you can "cold brew" a cup over night. The coffee needs to be refrigerated cold when creating the shake.

Pour all ingredients in the blender, blend until it is "milk shake" consistency.

Grab a spoon and a straw, pour into a glass, enjoy.

NOT FOR THE FAINT OF HEART
ICED COFFEE COCKTAIL

Not for the faint of heart, and another good title for this iced coffee should be "Happy Hour Special". This alcoholic beverage is only for adults due to the alcohol content. You do not want to start your day with this iced coffee.

However, this cool refreshing drink is perfect to chill, relax, and complete a day. Better to drink it right before or after dinner, so the caffeine will wear off by bedtime.

This drink certainly combines the hardcore coffee, espresso - with cocktail ingredients to make for an interesting iced coffee cocktail, a combination that grown-ups are sure to love.

Many iced coffees are created to the taste of the creator, so you need to put your thinking cap on with this one and add or take away as you please.

Remember, with iced coffee, anything goes. Just think about what you enjoy drinking and apply it to an iced coffee recipe.

This recipe is using cocktail ingredients. If you have other alcoholic beverages you would like to try with an iced coffee, go ahead, and try them, you may discover a new drink combination that can be a hit!

If you are a coffee lover that also enjoys your cocktails, this is the perfect beverage for you. Of course, you can vary it up by adding more vodka or Kahula if you want a stronger drink. You can add more espresso if you dare and you want more zing.

Ingredients:

- → **3/4 cup of coffee flavored vodka**
- → **1 tablespoon of Kahlua**
- → **1 tablespoon of espresso**
- → **4 coffee beans**
- → **Crushed ice**

Pour vodka and crushed ice in a cocktail shaker, and shake for half a minute.

Add in the Kahlua and the espresso and shake enough to mix well.

Allow to chill for about a minute.

Add a coffee bean to 2 cocktail glasses.

Pour / strain the mixture into the cocktail glasses. Enjoy.

Serves 2.

Basic FAST Iced Coffee

We have given the basic recipe for cold brewed iced coffee and even a recipe to make the cold brew in abundance for those who want to store it for up to three weeks. The instant coffee recipe is best made as you drink it, because it will not store well.

However, this recipe is for those who wants a simple glass of iced coffee without the wait and who may not have the time or inclination to create cold brewed coffee.

Cold brew coffee at the very least takes 8 to 10 hours to create. Instant coffee helps to create a fast iced coffee and you can vary the flavorings from milk, or add in other flavors, easy enough.

You can try chocolate syrup, caramel syrup, butterscotch syrup. Sprinkle some cocoa powder. Sprinkle some cinnamon. Swizzle with a cinnamon stick.

Swizzle it with a peppermint stick and in addition add in some chocolate syrup, for a chocolate mint delight. Add a dollop of whipped cream topping.

Ingredients:

- → **2/3 cup of milk (cold)**
- → **3 tablespoons of water (warm)**
- → **2 teaspoons of instant coffee powder**
- → **1 teaspoon of sugar**
- → **Ice (crushed or cubed)**

Place the coffee and warm water in a cup and stir well. Add sugar and stir. Alternatively, place in a lidded jar and shake until foamy.

Pour the contents over a tall glass of ice.

Pour the milk in, stir, enjoy.

1 serving.

Double or triple the recipe to make larger servings or to serve a couple more people.

Variations:

Add in some - chocolate syrup, caramel syrup, butterscotch syrup. Add some coffee creamer, or flavored coffee syrups.

Substitute the milk with half-and-half.

Substitute the milk and sugar with sweetened condensed milk.

Substitute the sugar with honey or a sugar substitute like Equal or Sweet N' Low or stevia.

ICED CREAMY MOCHA ESPRESSO

Many times these iced coffee recipes are delicious as desserts. They are rich and think. You could almost eat this iced Creamy Mocha Espresso in a bowl with a spoon.

This is such a recipe that needs a spoon and a straw to eat. This iced espresso will go well after dinner or as a midafternoon cool treat.

Using ice and a frozen dairy, like ice cream and yogurt, helps to make the iced part truly frozen. Add in some whipped cream and you are in for a delightful, creamy, rich, decadent frozen treat.

All you need to do is add a cherry on top, for good measure.

Ingredients:

- → **1 cup of vanilla frozen yogurt or ice cream**
- → **1/2 cup of espresso, made and chilled**
- → **1/2 cup of milk**
- → **1/4 cup of whipped cream (heavy cream)**
- → **6 tablespoons of chocolate syrup**
- → **1 tablespoon of sugar**
- → **Garnish of cocoa powder or chocolate curls or cinnamon to taste**

Prepare the espresso. Brewed espresso tastes best in this recipe.

Chill it in the refrigerator.

Pour the espresso, milk, and sugar in the blender and blend until well mixed.

Stir in the frozen yogurt or ice cream and blend well.

Pour the drink into too tall glasses (place glasses in the freezer for a nice frosty effect).

Put a dollop or two of whipped cream on top and garnish with your choice of cocoa powder, chocolate curls or cinnamon.

Makes 2 servings.

Variations:

Substitute the milk and sugar for sweetened condensed milk for an extra creamy and sweet treat.

Substitute chocolate syrup with caramel syrup or butterscotch syrup.

Substitute sugar with honey or a sugar substitute.

If you do not wish to have the caffeinated zing you get with espresso, substitute regular coffee for the espresso.

Mocha Coffee Cappuccino on Ice

Hard core coffee lovers venture out and drink espresso and cappuccinos for that extra yum, full-bodied coffee flavor and the extra punch of caffeine.

It is easy to take these hard-core coffee flavors and make them into an iced drink. If you already love iced coffees, you will love this.

If you have never tried iced coffees, but love espressos or cappuccinos, you will like this.

This is a perfect "pep" drink to start the day, to give you some energy from the caffeine jolt.

It makes a nice after dinner treat too, or an anytime treat if you are a diehard chocolate lover.

Ingredients:

→ 1 cup of espresso
→ 1/4 cup of half-and-half
→ 1 tablespoon of chocolate syrup
→ 4 or 5 ice cubes

Make the cup of espresso as you normally do, either fresh brewed or instant. Double espresso works well with this recipe, as does the real strong coffee.

The coffee or espresso needs to be nice and hot, not chilled.

Allow the chocolate syrup to drizzle into the cup while stirring the coffee, to help melt and blend into the hot coffee / espresso.

Pour the hot liquid into a blender, add the half-and-half, and ice cubes. Turn to high and blend for a couple of minutes.

Pour into a tall frosty glass (place glass in the freezer for about 10 minutes to make frosty).

Enjoy.

Serves 1.

If you'd like it to be a bit more icy, try adding in more ice cubes, and make the coffee or espresso a little stronger.

Variations:

Substitute the chocolate syrup for caramel syrup. On the other hand, add caramel syrup for an extra sweetness.

If you want to be doubly sweet, substitute the half-and-half with sweetened condensed milk.

Add a dollop of whipped topping if desired to the finished product.

Iced Mocha Coffee Frappe

This is an iced coffee version of the favorites of mocha and frappes. This is a perfect drink for coffee and chocolate lovers alike.

This drink is such a treat; it is easy to vary the recipe to create something new (just like with most all of the iced coffee recipes).

When you serve this recipe, it is best to have a tall spoon to dip, and a straw to slurp. You can drink this for breakfast or have it as an after dinner dessert.

Ingredients:

> → **Almost a full cup of cold coffee**
> **(make strong coffee and chill)**
> → **1/4 cup of chocolate syrup**
> → **20 ice cubes**
> → **2 teaspoons of vanilla**
> → **Whipped cream to garnish**

Prepare the coffee ahead of time make it extra strong by using double the amount of grounds. You can brew it, or make it from instant coffee powder.

Then chill the coffee completely in the refrigerator, until it is cold.

Pour the coffee, chocolate syrup, vanilla, and ice into a blender. Blend until ingredients are smooth texture.

Chill a tall glass in the freezer for about 10 minutes to make it nice and frosty, pour the blended drink into the frosted glass.

Place a dollop or two of the whipped cream on top. Enjoy.

Serves 1 tall glass (at least 16 ounces), or serves 2 cups if you want to share.

Better yet, double the recipe to make it for 2 and enjoy 2 full sized glasses.

Variations:

Turn it into a caramel coffee frappe by substituting caramel syrup for chocolate.

Make a "Caramel Mocha Coffee Frappe" by mixing in 1/8 cup of the chocolate syrup with 1/8 cup of caramel syrup.

Make a creamy vanilla frappe by substituting the chocolate syrup with sweetened condensed milk. Substitute whipped cream with ice cream. Garnish with chocolate curls, or cocoa or drizzle a little caramel or chocolate syrup.

Iced Thai Coffee

This is a delicious drink to have with a Thai meal or as a relaxing beverage at any time during the day. This iced coffee has a rich bold flavor, yet with a very sweet and spicy undertone.

Strong coffee is best enjoyed anytime during the day, but because of the high caffeine content, should not be drunk right before bedtime.

It is a good wake up drink, the flavor will wake up the taste buds and the strong coffee will wake the other senses.

Ingredients:

➔ **2 cups of brewed coffee (strong coffee, French roast works well or Colombian, keep it hot no need to chill)**
➔ **1 tablespoon of brown sugar**
➔ **1 tablespoon of sweetened condensed milk**
➔ **dash of ground cloves (to taste)**
➔ **dash of cinnamon (to taste)**
➔ **half and half to flavor (optional)**
➔ **crushed ice (enough to fill a tall glass)**

Make the coffee brew it strong. A French blend is good. Brewed coffee is best, but an instant coffee will work too, just make it strong.

While the coffee is still hot, blend in the brown sugar, sweetened condensed milk, ground cloves, and cinnamon until well mixed.

Meanwhile, chill a tall glass in the freezer for 10 minutes to give it a good frosting effect.

Fill the frosted glass with crushed ice, pour coffee mixture, and stir well.

Pour in half-and-half if desired. Enjoy.

1 serving.

If any coffee is left over, it is best stored in the refrigerator. Just add some ice to refresh and continue to enjoy the rich bold flavor later.

This recipe varies well if you wish to try different spices or flavorings. You can leave off the spices and use flavored syrups like chocolate and caramel. Substitute the brown sugar with granulated sugar, honey or a sugar substitute.

INSTANT CHOCOLATE ICED COFFEE

Sometimes you may just want to make a glass of iced coffee spontaneously and will not have the time to create the cold-brew method. This recipe is more of an instant method and perfect for those times when you want a glass of delicious iced coffee immediately without the wait. This recipe has no prep time; you simply make it when you want it. You just need to make sure you have ice and a blender.

Ingredients:

Mix in a bowl first

> ➜ **1/2 cup of warm water (filtered warm water is best)**
> ➜ **2 teaspoons of instant coffee (any brand - caffeinated or decaffeinated, it does not really matter as long as it is instant coffee)**

Then mix in a blender

> ➜ **the coffee mixture from above**
> ➜ **one tray of ice or about a dozen cubes from an automatic ice maker**
> ➜ **1/2 cup of milk**
> ➜ **5 ounces of sweetened condensed milk (like Eagle brand milk)**
> ➜ **1 tablespoon of chocolate syrup (Hershey's or any brand)**

Blend until the ice breaks up and the mixture is smooth and rich. Pour into tall glasses and enjoy.

Feel free to substitute the chocolate syrup with caramel or butterscotch syrup. You can find other flavors in the ice cream topping section at the grocery store.

You can vary this too and combine syrups. Try a chocolate caramel combination. On the other hand, a strawberry chocolate combination, etc.

The fun is to invent flavors. Try adding a scoop or two of vanilla ice cream for a frozen instant iced coffee treat. Play around with different flavors of ice cream that will go well with the choice of syrup and coffee.

If you add ice cream, the mixture will be thicker. You can also add some whipped topping to the glass after you pour the drink.

"Americano Caffe" Style Iced Coffee

When you wake up, do you enjoy a hot cup of coffee or do you make a nice tall glass of iced coffee? Sometimes iced coffee offers a tasty alternative to its steamy sister. In warmer weather and nice glass of refreshing iced coffee will hit the spot, especially if it has fresh citrus fruit added.

Many people will discover they will become an iced coffee maniac when they try it for the first time. Many coffee loving people will not try iced coffee because of the preparation time, or at the very least, they will not make it at home.

Many recipes call for a cold brew formula that requires overnight brewing. On the other hand, you have the instant coffee recipes, which if you are a brewed coffee snob, you will not care for instant anything coffee.

Then there are the true caffeine addicts who love coffee on steroids, - espresso. Espresso serves best in tiny shots, because it packs such a caffeinated punch. Imagine the punch of espresso in a delicious iced coffee recipe.

Ingredients

→ **2 shots of espresso**
→ **2 cups hot water (not boiling hot, just before it boils, steamy)**
→ **4 slices of lime (thin slices - 3mm)**
→ **4 slices of apricot (thin slices - 3mm)**
→ **1 tray of crushed ice cubes (or 12 crushed automatic ice maker ice cubes)**

First, make the coffee or espresso in this manner:

Heat the 2 cups of water to hot, not boiling.

Add the 2 shots of espresso to hot water.

Chill the coffee before creating the iced coffee.

Put 2 slices of lime and 2 slices of apricot into a tall glass.

Fill glass with crushed ice.

Pour espresso coffee over ice.

Makes 2 servings, so enjoy with a friend.

Spicy Cinnamon and Cardamon Iced Coffee

This iced coffee recipe is probably one of the least complicated around, because of the simplicity to create, and no need for overnight cold brewing.

Yes, it uses an instant coffee, but the spices help to give it a rich spicy flavor. In addition, you can sweeten it to your liking.

That is the beauty of iced coffee, the room for improvising. You can follow a recipe to a Tee if you want, but you do not have to.

You can improvise it. You can add in more ingredients, increase ingredients, decrease ingredients. Vary this recipe; try making it with two cups of hot brewed coffee instead of 3 tablespoons of instant coffee and 2 cups of water.

Try some cream, or milk, if you enjoy a creamier version. There is no one saying you cannot add a bit of whipped cream to the top once you pour your iced glass.

Try different additions and come up with a recipe that is unique to you. Or enjoy this as is, because either way, it is delicious.

The cardamom is a spice from India, and we all know how spicy foods are in India.

This spice adds extra zip with the cinnamon and the vanilla helps to balance the zip with smoothness.

Ingredients

> → **2 cups of water**
> → **3 tablespoons of your favorite instant coffee**
> → **Sugar to taste (start with 3 tablespoons and add more if needed)**
> → **1/4 teaspoon of cinnamon**
> → **1/4 teaspoon of cardamom**
> → **1 teaspoon of vanilla**

This is an easy recipe to fix.

Just dump all the ingredients into a saucepan big enough to hold them.

Heat on medium high, stirring constantly, until it foams. No need to sieve (instant coffee!).

Stir, pour over ice in tall glasses, enjoy!

CINNAMON HONEY ICED COFFEE

Sometimes, adding ice to coffee it can dilute the mixture and make it too watery. If you try a recipe and this occurs, next time you create the recipe, make the coffee a little stronger.

Iced coffee needs to be nice and cold, like a cold glass of iced tea. The ice should not melt fast. Pouring hot coffee over ice cubes will certainly dilute the coffee and will not be as cold.

When creating iced coffee it is important to allow enough time to cool the mixture down before pouring over ice. Put the hot mixture in a container in the refrigerator to cool it down properly before serving.

This is a very simple recipe of taking your average cup of coffee, and adding a few ingredients to make it into a delicious glass of iced coffee. If you want the recipe to be sweeter, add more honey.

Likewise if you want more cinnamon flavor, add a shake or two more of cinnamon. You may desire more milk, increase it.

Substitute the milk for half-and-half. If you are really into sweets, substitute the milk for sweetened condensed milk. Nevertheless, make sure you really like it sweet first.

Make this an allergy prevention beverage by using honey that was created in your local area. This is the best way to combat allergies too. If anyone asks what you are drinking, tell him or her it is an allergy prevention concoction.

Ingredients:

→ **2 cups of hot coffee (either brewed or instant)**
→ **half cup of milk**
→ **1/4 cup of honey**
→ **1/8 teaspoon of cinnamon**

Pour all ingredients in a saucepan and heat. Do not boil.

Stir often, mixture is done when it steams.

Allow to cool, pour over tall glass of ice.

Makes 2 servings.

Pina Colada Iced Coffee

Try to think of a warm tropical paradise with this delicious pina colada iced coffee recipe. You will be dreaming of a warm tropical beach as you sip this wonderful drink.

This iced coffee recipe is for adults only, since it calls for the alcoholic beverage rum. This iced coffee is best served after dinner and not as a breakfast drink. You can add more or less of the coconut cream or pineapple juice to your liking.

The drink can be made without the rum for a virgin pina colada iced coffee and to serve to those under age. Using fresh coconut "milk" or cream is best, but if you cannot find a fresh one, canned is okay, same with the pineapple juice and slices.

If it is not sweet enough, add some sugar, honey or sweetened condensed milk. The recipe is variable to create what you enjoy. It may be delicious to add some whipped topping and a cherry before serving.

Ingredients:

- ➔ **1 cup cold coffee**
- ➔ **4 tablespoons of light rum**
- ➔ **4 tablespoons of coconut cream**
- ➔ **2 tablespoons of pineapple juice**
- ➔ **2 slices of pineapple (fresh is best)**
- ➔ **Ice - crushed (as much as you like for one serving)**

Make coffee, either cold brew (which the coffee will have to "brew" overnight) or brew hot coffee and allow to cool, or use instant coffee. (You can also use the coffee called for in the Simple Cold Brew recipe found in this eBook too.)

Using blender, add all the ingredients and blend.

Place a pineapple slice on the side of a tall glass (like a lemon wedge or slice) and pour coffee mixture into glass. Enjoy.

(For fun, find a cute umbrella to decorate the drink.)

Double the recipe for two servings.

Iced Mint Mocha

This recipe is tailor made for those who are coffee and chocolate mint lovers. Many different flavors go well with chocolate and mint is no exception.

Experience the cool refreshing mint coupled with the decadence of chocolate and the strength of coffee in a rich creamy frozen dessert quality drink.

Grab your spoon and straw for this refreshing delight. This recipe lends itself to great variations, allowing you to create it with ease.

Coffee brings out the delicate taste of chocolate, which is why mocha (chocolate and coffee combined) is such a popular flavor.

Ingredients

> → **1/2 cup of coffee**
> → **1/2 cup of milk**
> → **1 scoop of chocolate ice cream**
> → **1 peppermint stick ***
> → **12 ice cubes**
> → **Whipped topping to garnish (optional)**
> → **Chocolate mints to garnish (optional)**

Make the coffee in one of your favorite fashions: fresh hot brewed or with hot water and instant coffee.

Cold brew will not work with this recipe since the hot coffee is needed to melt the peppermint stick.

While the coffee is still steaming hot, not boiling, add the peppermint stick and swizzle until melted.

Cool the coffee in the refrigerator.

Pour cold coffee and peppermint into a blender; add in the milk, chocolate ice cream, and ice.

Blend until smooth.

Pour into a tall frosty (chilled) glass. Add whipped topping if desired. Enjoy.

Serves 1.

> * Use a chalky peppermint stick for the best results. A candy cane will work. On the other hand, throw in 3 of the small peppermint candies (Star mints).

Variations:

Substitute 1 scoop of vanilla ice cream and 1 tablespoon of chocolate syrup for the chocolate ice cream.

Substitute half-and-half OR sweetened condensed milk for the regular milk, for a creamier drink.

Garnish with chocolate peppermints if you are a diehard chocolate mint lover.

CHERRY CORDIAL ICED COFFEE

This recipe plays on those who have an affinity for cherry cordials and the sweeter things in life. Have you ever drunk a cherry cordial? Who can resist the rich flavors of chocolate and cherry when you bite into a cherry cordial candy?

The creamy milk chocolate, the sweet cherry, the gooey sweet center, it is mouth-watering good, irresistible.

This cherry cordial drink is delicious hot or cold, but for this recipe will be set up for ice. You can enjoy this delicious drink as a dessert after supper; savor the sweet chocolate cherry flavor along with your coffee.

Grab your spoon and be prepared for a sweet cherry adventure.

Ingredients:

- ➜ **1 cup of coffee**
- ➜ **1/4 cup of condensed sweetened milk**
- ➜ **1/4 cup of milk**
- ➜ **2 tablespoons of chocolate syrup**
- ➜ **1 tablespoon of cherry juice**
(right from a jar of maraschino cherries) - add more cherry juice for a stronger cherry flavour
- ➜ **12 ice cubes**
- ➜ **whipped topping (as garnishment)**
- ➜ **1 cherry (as garnishment)**

Make your cup of coffee either from fresh brew, instant coffee or cold brew. Make sure the coffee is cold. Make it as strong as you like.

Frost a tall glass in the freezer for at least 10 minutes.

Cherry juice can come from a jar of maraschino cherries.

Pour the coffee, condensed sweetened milk, milk, chocolate syrup, cherry juice, and ice cubes into a blender, blend until smooth.

Pour into the tall frosted glass.

Top with whipped topping, add cherry on top. Enjoy.

Serves 1 large or 2 small drinks.

Variations:

For less sweet flavor, substitute the condensed sweetened milk with either half-and-half or regular milk.

Instead of whipped topping, try a scoop of vanilla ice cream.

Blend the vanilla ice into the mixture, for a thicker, creamier drink.

Basic Coffee Milkshakes - Vanilla, Rum or Chocolate

This basic coffee milkshake is definitely a dessert. Rich in coffee flavor, ice cream lovers will enjoy a frozen treat like this. Venture out and try some of the variations listed below the directions.

Coffee ice cream alone is very tasty, but when you add in more coffee and rum, you turn a tasty treat into a delectable dessert.

This is a perfect treat for those hot summer days. If you enjoy your coffee, but the heat makes a hot steamy cup of coffee undesirable, try the Basic Coffee Milkshake instead. You will be getting your fill of coffee flavor and the cool refreshing taste of frozen ice cream.

You can make this treat ahead of time and store in the freezer. In fact, this would be good to have in those tall glass mugs, so when you pull them from the freezer, they will be all frosty and make the treat all the more enjoyable.

Ingredients:

- ➔ **2 cups of coffee flavored ice cream**
- ➔ **5 scoops of vanilla ice cream**
- ➔ **1/2 cup of rum (optional)**
- ➔ **2 teaspoons of fine ground coffee**
- ➔ **Instant coffee**

To create a basic coffee milkshake, first add the coffee ice cream and the fine ground coffee (and the rum if you choose) into a blender, blend until smooth.

Pour mixture into a tall glass.

Add a scoop or two of the vanilla ice cream; spread some instant coffee over the vanilla scoops. Enjoy.

Variations:

Blend ALL the ingredients for an extra thick and rich coffee milk shake.

Make it a chocolate mocha by adding some chocolate syrup.

On the other hand, use chocolate ice cream instead of vanilla ice cream.

Add some caramel syrup.

Add both caramel and chocolate.

Top with whipped topping and a cherry.

Contact Information

I hope you like my book, you that you are enjoying the many different recipes.

You can always visit my coffee website www.coffee-makers-review.com,

Here you will find a vast number of reviews on all the latest coffee makers, as well as tips on making coffee, espresso, latte macchiato and so on.

You can contact me with queries at coffee11@coffee-makers-review.com

Made in the USA
Las Vegas, NV
25 November 2021

35257024R00026